I Wonder What It's Like to Be a Butterfly

Erin M. Hovanec

The Rosen Publishing Group's

PowerKids Press™

New York

*To my Mom, Mary Ellen Hovanec, in celebration of a year of
wonderful changes and metamorphoses.*

Published in 2000 by The Rosen Publishing Group, Inc.
29 East 21st Street, New York, NY 10010

Photo Credits: p. 3 © F.P.G./Gail Shumway; p. 4 © F.P.G./Telegraph Colour Library; pp. 5, 7 © F.P.G./Gail Shumway; p. 8 © Don Riepe/Peter Arnold, Inc., © Animals, Animals/E. R. Degginger, © Animals, Animals/Patty Murray; p. 11 © Animals, Animals/Carol Geake, © F.P.G./Peter Gridley, © James L. Amos/Peter Arnold, Inc., © Animals, Animals/Eastcot/Momatiuk, p. 12 © WHM Bildarchiv/Peter Arnold, Inc., © Animals, Animals/Nancy Rotenberg; p. 15 © Animals, Animals/Patti Murray; p. 16 © Animals, Animals/George Bryce, © F.P.G./Telegraph Colour Library; p. 19 © Animals, Animals/Breck P. Kent; p. 20 © Animals, Animals/E. R. Degginger, © Animals, Animals/ Carroll W. Perkins, © Hans Pfletschinger/Peter Arnold, Inc.; p. 22 © Lior Rubin/Peter Arnold, Inc.

Photo Illustrations by Thaddeus Harden

First Edition

Book Design: Felicity Erwin

Manufactured in the United States of America

Contents

Beautiful Butterflies

Where have you seen butterflies? Flying happily from flower to flower through forests and fields? Lying lazily on rocks, flapping their pretty wings and enjoying sunny afternoons? Seems like an easy life, right? Did you know, though, that some butterflies have to **hibernate** for months every winter? Did you know that they fly thousands of miles with those beautiful wings? Did you know that those pretty colors help protect them from their enemies? What would it be like to be a butterfly?

◀ *The life of a butterfly isn't always as easy as it seems.*

5

Little Bodies, Big Wings

Can you imagine finding a butterfly as big as a bird? Well, some are. There are 20,000 **species** of butterflies, and they come in all different sizes. The smallest are only the size of a dime, and the largest are much bigger. Some butterflies' wings measure almost a foot across.

Like all **insects**, a butterfly's body has three parts. The first, its head, includes the butterfly's eyes, mouth, and **antennae**, or feelers. The butterfly uses its antennae to smell, hear, and touch. The second section is the **thorax**. The butterfly's wings and legs are attached to the thorax. A butterfly has two pairs of wings, a front pair and a back pair. It also has six legs. The **abdomen**, the last section, has important body parts inside it that help the butterfly **reproduce** and **digest** food.

A butterfly's wings are many ▶
times the size of its body.

8

Amazing Changes

Did you know that a butterfly starts its life as a caterpillar and then changes into a butterfly? This **metamorphosis**, or change, may seem magical to people. For a butterfly, though, it's just a natural part of life.

A butterfly starts life as a tiny egg. When the egg hatches, a **larva**, or caterpillar, crawls out. In a few weeks, the caterpillar gets very big, sometimes hundreds of times its original size. When it sheds its skin, it becomes a **chrysalis**. A chrysalis is a hard shell with a caterpillar inside. As time passes, maybe a few days or maybe a year, the caterpillar starts to change form. It is becoming a butterfly. Finally, the newborn butterfly breaks out of its shell, stretches its wings, and sets off to explore the world.

◀ *A butterfly is a caterpillar, then a chrysalis, before it finally grows its beautiful wings.*

All Around the World

Butterflies exist almost everywhere in the world. Some butterflies like to live in hot, dry deserts. Some love wet, dark jungles, and others make their homes in meadows filled with flowers. Most butterflies especially like warm, damp places. More butterflies live in tropical areas than anywhere else.

One thing that butterflies don't like is rain. This is because the wetness and weight of the rain can damage their wings. When it rains, they hide under leaves or near rocks. No one, including butterflies, wants to be caught in a rainstorm!

Butterflies live in all different places. ▶

11

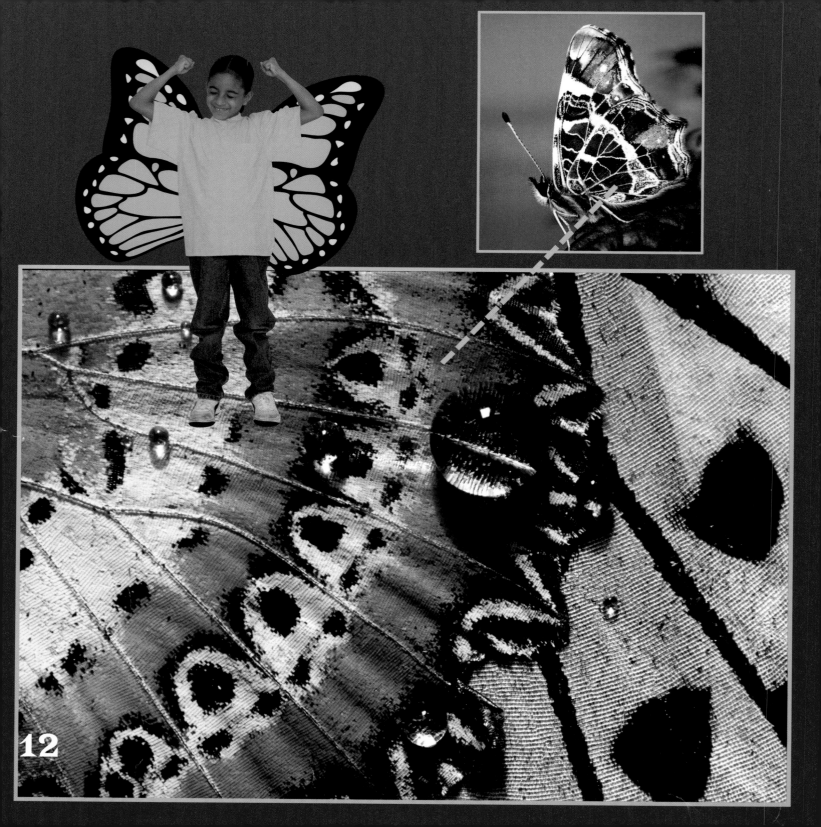

Pretty but Powerful

Scientists believe that butterflies have existed for about 48 million years. Butterflies may look delicate, but they're very strong.

A butterfly's strength also helps it fly high in the air. A butterfly's wings have **veins**. Air runs through these veins and helps the wings keep their shape. The outer part of the wing is flexible. When the butterfly flaps its wings, the flexible part bends and pushes the air backward. This is how the butterfly moves forward. The front part of the wing is stiff, and helps the butterfly lift into the air. People have seen butterflies flying above buildings that are over a thousand feet tall. That's almost 100 stories high!

◀ *The veins that run through a butterfly's wings are filled with air. They help the wings keep their shape.*

Braving the Cold

Most butterflies don't like cold weather. Those who live in cold climates often find warm, safe places to hibernate, or go into a deep sleep, during the winter. They choose a cozy spot that protects them from cold, wind, and snow. Butterflies use trees, leaves, logs, and just about anything else that will give them shelter. **Chemicals** in their bodies help them to stay alive by protecting them from the cold and keeping them from getting hungry.

Other butterflies **migrate** to warm places to escape the cold. To migrate means to move from one area and settle in another. Monarch butterflies are famous for their migrations. They travel in huge groups. Monarchs travel a large distance. They often travel as far as 2,000 miles from home. For you, that would almost be like walking across the United States!

When monarchs migrate, there can be so many ▶
of them that the butterflies look like a cloud.

15

A monarch
caterpillar
eating a leaf

16

Finding Food

If you were a butterfly, your favorite food would be a tasty substance called **nectar**. Nectar is a sweet and sugary liquid found inside flowers. Butterflies spend their lives flying from one flower to another drinking up the nectar.

When young butterflies are still caterpillars, they eat mostly green plants. Caterpillars' mouths have jaws that help them to chew pieces of plant. They eat a lot of food because they're hungry all the time. Caterpillars spend most of their lives eating. In a single day, a caterpillar can eat several times more than it weighs!

◀ *Butterflies visit flowers for their nectar.*

Using Their Smarts

Lots of insects and animals, such as flies, wasps, and birds, eat butterflies. These animals are **predators**, or animals that live by eating or attacking other animals. Many butterflies and caterpillars use **protective coloration** to blend in with their surroundings and escape their predators. Butterflies that spend a lot of time on the ground are brown, like soil, and those who live in trees are green, like leaves. That way, enemies don't see them. Wouldn't it be neat to blend into your surroundings?

Other butterflies defend themselves by smelling or tasting bad. Bad-tasting butterflies have a certain pattern on their wings, called warning coloration. The colors warn predators that the butterfly won't taste good, so they don't bother it.

This is a dead leaf butterfly. It is brown so it ▶ blends in with the dead leaves of trees.

19

Owl Butterfly

Tropical Satyr

Wood Nymph

20

Butterfly Family Facts

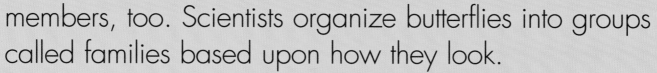

Do you look like anyone in your family? Maybe you have hair like your mom or dad's. Butterflies look like their family members, too. Scientists organize butterflies into groups called families based upon how they look.

One butterfly family, the satyr and wood nymph family, has special markings called eyespots. Eyespots are markings that look like eyes. Since they fly very close to the ground, satyrs and wood nymphs have brown wings to help them blend into the soil. The eyespots draw enemies' attention to their wings so they will be less likely to hurt more important parts of the butterfly's body.

All three of these butterflies have eyespot markings on their wings. They seem to be looking right at you!

Many, Many More

Can you imagine tasting food with your feet instead of your mouth? That's what brush-footed butterflies do. They have tiny front legs called brush feet. These legs have special **sensory** parts that help butterflies sense when food is near.

Butterflies can do all sorts of interesting things. They live everywhere and come in every size and color. It might be nice to be a butterfly.

Glossary

abdomen (AB-duh-min) The last of the three parts of an insect's body.

antennae (an-TEH-nee) Feelers on the head of a butterfly that the butterfly uses to smell, hear, and touch.

chemical (KEM-ih-kuhl) A substance with specific traits that is made from a combination of elements.

chrysalis (KRIH-suh-luhs) The hard shell a caterpillar forms when it changes to a butterfly.

digest (dy-JEST) To change food into energy the body can use.

hibernate (HY-behr-nayt) To go into a deep sleep, often during the winter.

insects (IN-sekts) Small animals that have six legs, like butterflies.

larva (LAHR-vah) The stage of a butterfly's life when it is a caterpillar.

metamorphosis (meh-tuh-MOR-fuh-sis) A change of form.

migrate (MY-grayt) To move from one place to settle in another.

nectar (NEKT-ar) Sweet liquid found inside flowers.

predators (PREH-da-torz) Animals that live by eating or attacking other animals.

protective coloration (pro-TEHK-tiv kuh-luh-RAY-shun) Body coloring that helps an animal blend in with its surroundings and stay safe from enemies.

reproduce (ree-PROH-doos) To make more of something.

sensory (SEN-sor-ee) Having to do with sensation or the senses.

species (spee-SHEES) A group of animals which have many things in common.

thorax (THOR-aks) The second of the three parts of the body of an insect.

veins (VAYNZ) Small vessels that allow the transportation of a substance in a living thing.

Index

Web Sites:

You can learn more about butterflies on the Internet. Check out these Web sites:

http://www.mesc.usgs.gov/butterfly/Butterfly.html

http://www.butterflyfarm.co.cr/farmer/bfly1.htm